HUMANITY THE FUTURE REPORT

SHORT AND BRIEF

ENNIS C. JACKSON

outskirts
press

This book is dedicated to the former, present, and future leaders of every country. It is dedicated to every person and everything that we call Life. It is dedicated to believers and nonbelievers of what some call a higher Holy or non-Holy power. It's dedicated to the one ultimate leader of this world, as time will reveal a change in direction for the future of mankind and the rest of life that flourishes on Earth. This book is dedicated to Nikkie.

Copyright

Terms and Conditions

The information provided is my opinion as to the value of your decision regarding the future, racism, security, building, space exploration, spending, training, transportation, care of the people of Earth, and the continued survival of our race and the organic life that flourishes within. You may consider additional matters after consulting with your scientific community before taking a specific course of action, which could unquestionably influence your success and limit errors that are bound to occur.

Results

The accounts that I will be talking about came from research and my personal knowledge as well as people whom I know and knew. Some of the people are acquaintances from visiting numerous places in the United States, Alaska, Japan, Philippines, Korea, and Mexico. Some others are family members from generations of names. Their stories were handed down from family to family and go as far back as the seventeenth century. However, my most compelling information came from some of my patients who were on the doorstep of death. They are the young and old who validated happiness, fear, longing, anger, acceptance, and finally having the strength to say "good-bye." To further elaborate the information for this book, the Internet with its free knowledge was assembled.

Table of Contents

Important Notice

ACCORDING TO THE scientists of the world, **Life** is referred to as the physiological functions of respiration, metabolism, and reproduction, in every existing thing. It could be the smallest microscopic life form, or it could be a tree, a leaf, grass, or intelligent life, such as humans. Is this a fluke, or is this the true nature of God, as he strategically placed life in the third world, situated in the Milky Way Galaxy and surrounded by, so far, a lifeless universe as we know it—or at least, what we are being told to believe. Nonetheless, you can call it fate, luck, destiny, opportunity, chance, or whatever you choose. The fact is, we are breathing, thinking, hurting, crying, talking, inventing, building, walking, running, playing, and continuing to reproduce. This activity makes us alive and well. But are we well?

The question should be whether we afford to continue to live here in this third world with a life that gets bombarded with the hazardous creations of nature and the inventions of humanity. We breathe in toxins that later permeate and transform into a kind of cancer or bacteria that deteriorates our cells to the point of a painful death. We eat food that is processed or even grown in a garden exposed to a free-flowing cosmic smorgasbord of slow growing, single- and multi-cell bacteria that will later mutate and **kill** us in a painful, agonizing death.

Oh! Don't stop here. What about terrorists, traffic collisions, and the penetration of projectiles, knives, and other traumatic objects brought upon us by accident, criminals, and future criminals? Indeed, some of this is voluntary, but the natural occurrences of nature take its toll on the human body as well, in the form of the disease, the wind, rain, lightning, floods, tornadoes, hurricanes, and the damaging effects of the sun from a manmade, slowly vanishing ozone layer. All of these effects cause us to seek the attention of professionals that specialize in every aspect of medicine and law enforcement along with scientists, teachers, clergy, and more. These professionals are people just like you and I, who for the most part don't work for free. These people have bills to pay, just like everybody else. Will they do it for free? Let us talk about that later, but for now, we shall move on.

Health Care

RECENTLY, HEALTH CARE was made available and is now reachable for so many people who are in need of it. This health care is called the Affordable Care Act, and it provides for all kinds of people, including the homeless and unfortunate, the people below minimum wage, the people above minimum wage, the below-comfortable people, the comfortable people, the above-comfortable people, the below-rich people, the rich people, and this is where it stops! Anybody above this level can probably start his or her insurance company and provide for every member of their family tree. Will they do this?

Unfortunately, resistance seems to be a factor in everything we do. When you have someone brave enough to make a stand to create **HELP** for the people of a nation or the people of the world, you have people arguing against him or her. Why does this happen? What is the issue? How do we go about resolving it? Once we resolve it, where do we go from there?

In my opinion, the answers are easy, and all it takes is action without resistance. Even more, it will take a skilled leader to step into the brightest light where everyone in the entire world can see him or her and hear what is said. It has been done before. Can it be done again? Let us start at the top.

Some Congress members and many others are against the Affordable Care Act for various reasons. Some are legitimate, and some are not. However, with all of the bickering and arguing that the Affordable Care Act will not work and is harmful to the people of America, there are many who have found the benefit of being able to see a doctor and get treatment for ailments that could have possibly killed him or her.

So, for those congress members and other citizens of America who argue against the plan, what are your alternatives? If you don't have one, then why fight against someone who is trying to improve health care affordability? It appears that you are simply making an argument based on your party and traits, not based on the welfare of the people.

For a country that boasts of being the most powerful nation in the world, it seems that we are not very smart and fall far behind other countries that are weaker but treat their citizens better concerning survival. Let us look at America's hospital saturation status and try to get a clearer idea of why the Affordable Care Act is necessary.

When a 911 call comes into the dispatch center for medical aids, EMTs, paramedics, and sometimes the fire department respond. Regardless of what the 911 call is for, there are usually medical complaints not relayed to the dispatcher. So, when the EMS team arrives and does an assessment, anything, including minor ailments to major life-threatening events, could be presented. For the most part, minor ailments turn out to be the majority reason for the emergency call.

A Primary Care Physician (PCP), or an Urgent Care Clinic (UCC) can easily manage these minor illnesses. Many people who call 911 asked about their choice versus the nonemergency route. Most indicated that they could not afford a PCP because they didn't have insurance. Others, including those who can afford a PCP, choose 911 because they believed that they could be seen much quicker, rather than have to sit in the waiting room for hours.

For those who drive themselves to the emergency room with these minor ailments, they find it unacceptable to sit in the waiting room for hours just to get a bed and be told by a doctor to take Tylenol or cough medicine for a common cold. As more people arrive at practically all of these emergency rooms around the country, the capacity becomes overwhelming as it turns out to be standing room only because all of the emergency room beds are taken.

Now, when you add the major emergencies that walk into the emergency rooms and are brought in by Emergency Medical Services (EMS), the problem of available beds causes that hospital to go on saturation or bypass. This bypass means that EMTs and paramedics will divert to another hospital, which is perhaps also on saturation. This bypass also means that the EMS team will be on an offload delay because the patient remains on their gurney until taken over by a nurse.

When EMS has to sit at the hospital for more than thirty minutes, it leaves a gap in the 911 system. Therefore, patients who call 911 will have to wait for an ambulance from a distance, or wait until one becomes available, regardless of the condition that patient may be in. That patient could be in a very serious condition or near death and their condition could be corrected by an EMS team. So, what can we do about this? What are our alternatives?

It seems that, whatever we do, the problem of health care will always be a major issue in every political party's pocket. The Affordable Health Care Act is a start and is certainly better than doing nothing. However, it could use a little extra help from private ambulance services.

Currently, this nation educates a great number of nurse practitioners (NP) and physician assistants (PA). They spend two to four years in college to achieve their credentials. Paramedics are not allowed to suture, write prescriptions, or order x-rays and laboratory tests; NPs and PAs can, and will be able to treat a patient in the patient's home. Most importantly, these healthcare personnel can recommend a follow up with the patient's physician or with a UCC for those patients who don't have a doctor.

In major metropolitan cities, the 911 system is so overwhelmed that the dispatcher cannot spend much time talking on the phone. This lack of time means that the call will be placed on hold, and it could be for an extended period, based on the urgency of the other calls. Here is where the dispatcher could refer the call to a private provider where these PAs and NPs will be sent to treat the patient. If the patient needs to be transported, a transport unit should be dispatched based on the patient's acuity; with this system in place, transport should be down to a low percentage.

The NPs and PAs who graduate from school should have a requirement of spending two years on an ambulance with these private providers. These NP's and PA's can also respond to patients addresses or locations in a certified emergency vehicle, other than an ambulance, where transport may not always be necessary. Of course, a trivial financial, governmental incentive, along with full compensation with benefits from the providing company, should be included. Furthermore, every city should be required to have these services in place.

Medical emergencies are usually not planned, and since they

take us by surprise, we should have the accommodations to handle them. These suggestions will work by eliminating waiting times in the emergency rooms for patients and EMS personnel, freeing 911 dispatchers to handle true emergencies, freeing EMS crews to also handle real emergencies, augmenting the Affordable Health Care Act by making follow-up visits reachable for patients, and recognizing cancer and diseases that are treatable when identified. So, how can we do this?

As usual, we have to start at the top. Governments should make it law for cities to have the field PA and NP system in place. Moreover, we must all agree to avoid any bickering, but you know how that goes. There always seems to be somebody who wants to argue about something. Unfortunately, those people are often in high places and have the power of the pen.

This system can also identify those people who escaped the opportunity to have medical insurance. With each field NP and PA call, time must be taken to enroll those who are not insured. Can you imagine the success it would be for private and government providers, as well as patients, financially? And let's not forget the health wise benefit the tax revenue would create because of the majority or all of the population insured? The national debt would certainly decrease. Let's give it a try!

Barack Obama

THE UNITED STATES has come a long way since those diabolical days of slavery. The rights of black people and women were absent, and looking back through the mirror of time, the country should have been ashamed of itself. Later, opportunities for African Americans and women emerged. Equality was met, but subtly; still, we are missing that 100 percent mark. We have a melting pot of nationalities in Congress, the Senate, Governors, Mayors, City Council Members, and ultimately, the President of the United States of America. It wasn't easy, and with every step came resistance.

Our current President Barack Obama is nearing the end of his two-term election years. Many of his predecessors did what they could while running the country. Each one of them inherited the leftovers of political instability in the country and around the world. Promises were made during the election phase, and some people believed everything that was said. But you know as well as I do that promises are hard to keep, especially when the situation changes. Because of the unfulfilled promises, these predecessors, and Barack Obama, will be one of those past leaders who the public refers to as prevaricators. We must understand that it is not the fault of the elected official.

With Barack Obama, a milestone of history was made and doubled when he won a second term. However, those who have issues with his policy projected their emotions through the media circuit and on the social networks. Some labeled President Obama as "the worst president this country has ever had." Mind you, most of those people were motivated by a political agenda that has much to do with being elected into office. Some are members of a racist group where his and her secret pointed hat is tucked away, but not thrown away. I would request that these people use caution in their statements because the country has not completely abolished racism, and this fringes on the absolute edge of inequality, jealousy, greed, and blatantly stating the untruth just to make one look bad, and yourself look good. People are getting tired of this, and it does not work anymore.

When you take a trip back through time, you will see that every president of this country had issues that dealt with foreign and local policy. None have endured the advanced impact and capability of the terrorists of today, other than President Barack Obama and George W. Bush. On top of that, President Obama worked on some of the promises he made while campaigning; some included the Affordable Health Care Act. Can you believe that politicians had issues with this?

When President Bush was in office, he endured the same issues, and one of them emerged with unparalleled success. The country was attacked in broad daylight. This violence appeared to have taken President Bush by surprise, and some people took issue with that. Why? President Bush, although the most powerful leader at that time, was still a man and subject to the same feelings and reactions as you and I, time can be on your side if you allow it to be. When he gathered his thoughts, he took action to mitigate the cause of the threat, and some people took issue with that. What does this all mean? It is simple. You can't please everybody. President Bush also incurred the headaches of medical care and joblessness in the United States. The guy was not perfect, and neither is Barack Obama, and neither are you.

Over the years, many politicians had opportunities to do something good about the many Americans who could not afford to see a doctor. Many people died because of trauma, heart conditions, and cancer that could have been treated if found early. The simple fact is that politicians do more talking than taking action to fix the problem. Let me give you an example.

In the news, we read and heard about the tobacco industry's take on people who died from cancer received from smoking cigarettes. Billions of dollars were paid out and yet cigarettes are still being made and sold. Now you know that money has a lot to do with it, and if cigarettes were removed from the world, a huge economic gap would develop and cause the rich to start renting. In other words, no more money will be made, and the money that was made went into the pockets and bank vaults of politicians. You know, the ones who vote and decide what we get to do or not do. Unfortunately, those who smoke cigarettes for a significant amount of time have problems stopping because of the addicting effects of the nicotine.

Yes, we have treatments for that but for some, it is too late. For others who want to quit, willpower gives in to buying more cigarettes because they are still on the shelf. The opportunities are still there. To fix the problem, it seems that all we have to do is stop making them. Yet, we have these politicians and people running for office who badmouth the person who is currently in office because Americans and other people around the world are still suffering and dying from cancer. We must understand that one person is not the cause of these leftover political issues. The blame falls on everyone who can vote and make a decision. Quite frankly, I am sick and tired of hearing quotes such as, "This is the worst president we have ever had," "lying Hillary," or "lying Ted," or "little Rubio," and even more. This behavior is not being an adult! This behavior is being childish and shows the world that the people of the most powerful nation on the planet are a bunch of whining babies. Is this our way of showing maturity? What the hell!

Barack Obama was not the worst president this nation has ever had. There has never been "the worst president this nation has ever had," including President Nixon. He just got caught. There are those who do a marvelous job, and there are those who don't do a marvelous job. However, the job that he or she does or will eventually do will be sufficient and organized. We must understand that one man or one woman does not have all the answers. Those come from advisors, brainstorming, and even from family members. But that doesn't always mean that the answer will be the right one. Sometimes we have to learn by trial and error, and this country and other countries around the world have been doing so for centuries.

The bottom line is simple: we as Americans and citizens of other countries must respect the person who we put into office. If it turns out that we lose faith in this person, we have the opportunity to change it by election. But during the term of that person, we must show respect and not insult or bully him or her personally or publically. When we use this form of respect, it shows maturity, that we have the ability to restrain ourselves, and that we are patient. Remember, if we put someone into office, and that person doesn't do what we want, it is our fault. So, when we say something derogatory about that person, we are saying something derogatory about ourselves.

Hillary Clinton

IT IS CLEAR that this nation has stepped further in equality. We now have a woman who is the nominee for the Democratic party. This should be an example as to the direction the country, and as well, the world, is going in regard to racism and equality. With Barack Obama and Hillary Clinton as examples of a changing society, our world's eyes need to be opened wider. But they are not. There are still areas of concern where women, blacks, Latinos and other races are maltreated. Even more, Hillary Clinton's quest to become the first female to lead the most powerful nation in the world has a foreseeable future that positions her in the same place as Barack Obama.

Skeptics and people who simply want to create an argument will introduce errors and blame them on Hillary Clinton, just as they did with Barack Obama. Once again, we have what we call childish behavior that portrays a vision of unrest and disrespect for a position that demands it, based on images set forth by our forefathers. Moreover, there are some who are not comfortable with Hillary Clinton becoming president. Some are active and former members of the military, specifically regarding the incident in Benghazi.

Benghazi enlightened a tail of errors that occurred and cost the lives of brave Americans. Decisions that should have been made were not, but do we know the reason behind it? Surely some things are not supposed to be brought to light because if they were, our national security could be threatened. Is this one of them? Well, until classified information becomes declassified, knowing may take a lifetime. So, is Hillary Clinton fit to lead this nation?

Hillary Clinton was the First Lady; she's educated, she was born in the United States, and she was Secretary of State. Of course she is fit to lead this nation, just like any one of us born in the USA who has the will and capability to do so. Our biggest problem as humans is being judgmental.

An argument could be brought forth regarding Hillary Clinton's husband, former President Bill Clinton. Well, a wise man or woman could ask, what does Bill Clinton's past events have to do with Hillary Clinton running for President of the United States today? Here is a good response: that is none of your business, and it has nothing to do with what one individual has to do with another. Surely by the religious laws of the land and everywhere else, when a man and a woman join in marriage, they become one. This statement happens to be true but not in every aspect.

Bill Clinton was a smart man. He was also a man of wisdom with traits that dates back to his childhood and teenage years. What he engaged in at that time was acceptable by some but not all. What he engaged in while in office was not acceptable, mainly because he was and is a married man who should have shown unbreakable morals. He is also a man who is subject to the same temptations of other men. But because of his weaknesses, does Hillary have to pay the price? The answer is no.

Each one of us is different. We have our own individual heart and brain. What we do, regardless of being married, does not reflect on our spouse, unless the spouse plays a part in the immoral mis-judgment. According to record, Hillary did not have knowledge of his activities until it matured in the media circuit—although, some of his activities are hearsay. What is impressive, unless there is something I don't know, is that Hillary remained faithful and by his side during the whole ordeal. I know it may have a bit to do with the fact that both are national icons, but there was nothing keeping her from telling Bill to take a hike.

If you look at the reasons people get a divorce in the United States, what sits on the top of the list is financial instability and infidelity. Financial instability is probably not the issue with the Clintons. Hillary showed great restraint and resolve. It could have been because she wanted to seek further employment with the government or it could have been that she simply wanted to keep the family together and forgave him. Or, it could have been both. It is not unheard of to forgive someone for moments of weakness.

So, Hillary Clinton deserves the same opportunities as anybody else as she seeks the highest office in the land. She has shown extreme determination, especially in the eyes of aggressive opponents with teeth as sharp as knives. What is obviously clear is that Hillary Clinton is not afraid of them, which is an indication that she will take on any challenge that presents itself before her. So, adversaries of the United States, beware! Hillary Clinton is no pushover and if you attempt to challenge her ability to respond after you knock that stick off of her shoulder, standby! You will have angered a powerful female giant.

Should Hillary fail to be elected President of the United States of America, any women can follow her shoes and perhaps win the election. Hillary Clinton is a great person and a woman of spirit. I like her and so should you.

Donald Trump

WHAT MAKES A rich man or women richer are not their traits, the way they talk, or pure luck. What makes a rich man or women richer is their elegance. Surely some of it comes from their background and family inheritance, but knowing how to make money is not something that every human being knows how to do.

Donald Trump has proven to the world that he is able to make and keep making money. His understanding of the business of making money is recognized worldwide. Moreover, Donald Trump can show people how to make money, and help them do so. He has proven that he can successfully run multiple genres of businesses. But does Mr. Trump know how to run a country?

Donald Trump has mentioned that he is not a politician but a businessman who has every right to make a bid for the highest office in the land. Although his motivation for running for office may be questionable, his determination is genuine. He portrays the vision of a man who can do anything if you give it a try. He also appears to comprehend the necessities of advisors who will assist him when making decisions about foreign or local policy. After all, that's why they are there. But will Mr. Trump listen to his advisors and take heed to their suggestions about other areas of presidential responsibility, such as the needs of the military and foreign policy?

Mr. Trump has, several times, responded to attacks against his pomposity and policy on immigrants and Muslims. It appears that he is making a speech without studying the ramifications of the impact it would have on his campaign, immigrants, and Muslims. He mentions Muslims, but in his language, there is no indication that he is referring to all of them. I believe he is referring to the Muslims who are here illegally that are crossing the borders unchecked.

Mr. Trump has mentioned the word radical, but so have Hillary Clinton, President Obama, and numerous other major figures. Let us not get into semantics, and clearly, understand that a word does not make a person who he or she is. You can call terrorists anything you want, but to major figures' the actions of terrorist determine and describe their motivation. But if we were to use the word radical and direct it toward a certain person or group of people, let us say that immigration and crossing the border unchecked is just a small part of the problem.

The people who identify themselves as radicals are associated with the term "terrorist." Well, terrorists are typically known as foreigners, but some are born in the United States, England, Spain, Portugal, Japan, Korea, and every other nation. So, if terrorists are born in every nation and are brought up to cause mass destruction, how can you keep them out, if they are already in?

Other aspects of Mr. Trump's magniloquence are that he appears to speak incompletely. It doesn't make him wrong or right but simply identifies his preference in communication. When speaking to graduates from college, some have an understanding of what he is saying. However, for undergraduates and high school students, Mr.

Trump speaks in parables. Although he seems authentic, he does not complete a sentence that gives a definable meaning. He goes from one interesting subject without an end and opens up another and yet that one is incomplete. Although, ultimately, he completes them all.

Donald Trump is an educated man with an impeccable resume. His bid for president of the United States is difficult but could be easier by responding in a nonbiased manner to the events that occur in the United States and around the world. Instead of saying that President Obama doesn't like him for believing or saying something opposite of what most people believe, he should say, "My heart grieves for all of the people whose lives were lost or affected by this tragedy. Although President Obama and I have our differences, we both agree on this one thing: this has got to stop, and if I am elected president of the United States of America, I will meet with my military and law-enforcement advisors to formulate a plan to handle the gun violence that seems to keep happening in this great land that we call home."

As President of the United States, Prime Minister, President of Russia, and other countries, the people have high regard for your ability to solve problems. We know that you are human and that time is not always your friend. But, do your best and portray a leader who is patient and takes the time to think before making a decision. Use your assets to gain the upper hand against your adversaries, but move swiftly to show that you will not tolerate violence against any of your citizens.

As the world turns, so does time, so how do we learn new ways of handling situations with each rotation? Leaders have what it takes to make a difference. But for each leader and future leader, hold your hands together as if you were filling them with water. Imagine that instead of water, you have the whole world in your hands. What happens to it depends on the choices you make and how you respond to threats.

With Donald Trump, he may win the electoral college vote. However, the popular vote may think differently, but the people of America will read this book and see that we have to show the world that we respect anyone who wins the office of the President of the United States of America.

Terrorist

YOU WERE BORN into this world as a human being. Your appearance resembles that of every man, woman, and child who thrives and relishes each morning and each night. You eat and drink the same way as everybody else. You bathe and walk just like everybody else. Although your language is different, you speak with intelligence, which means that you learn just like everybody else. But you are different in the way that you believe.

As a child, you were taught to believe that some people are considered to be infidels because they do not believe in the religious ways of your teaching. Over the years, you learn to hate those infidels and are trained in ways that are forbidden by every form of society. You smile when the blood of what you call infidels is spilled on the streets, yet that same smile vanishes when that blood turns out to be your own. What does this mean?

Tears are for eyes and moans are for cries. You see this, and you hear this coming from every nation, including your own. Are you trying to mimic the barbaric behavior of ancient history's past? Or, are you so heartless that you don't care about life itself? Apparently, to prove a point, you are willing to take your life. So, if you are dead, you won't know the outcome. This action that you take boggles some of the greatest minds. But is it necessary? The answer is no.

Your hate for these so-called infidels is the same as hating humanity, including your own. There is no need to get rid of them because the future is coming and you will need them. However, presently, you are a danger to a peaceful world. Your actions are frightening, but just like an Eagle, the double-headed Eagle, the Three-Lions Crest, and every nation's symbol, and the cat that gets cornered against a wall, standby! That cat will not sit there and let you tear him apart. He will fight back with every ounce of strength he has. Although he knows the end may be near, his zest for life far outweighs your attempts to take his away.

So, speak to the leaders of the world and have a peaceful conversation. Tell them why you are so angry. Tell them what compels you to commit atrocious crimes and give your life as a sacrifice, for surely the ultimate sacrifice occurs when you die defending your family and the country you love. Hopefully, a resolve can be reached, because the crimes that you commit must come to an end. It must stop! You are only attacked because you are attacking!

If you look at the earth from space, you can see one obvious image. Do you know what that is? Well, let me tell you. It is a blue planet that is flourishing with life. It is just one planet where all of us live. If you think about it, we all call this planet home. Every one of us calls this planet home. Is it possible to get along in our home?

For those who follow such a violent way of life, please take a moment and consider the realities of your actions. Converting to radical behavior is a choice and is misread in all interpretations of what you call a religious book. You are allowing yourself to become psychotic to the point where you are blind and deaf. Simply open your eyes and take a moment to hear the heartbeats of the men, women, and the little children around you. They are you, and you are them: humans, who are flourishing. So please, stop the violence.

There is no sense in taking your life to prove a point. Think about it. You blow yourself up with a vest bomb just to kill many other people. Can't you see that your purpose is not served? No! It looks like you can't see it because you are dead. If you gave it just a little bit of thought, you would see that there are other ways of achieving what you need and what your intended goals are. Taking a more peaceful route will enable you to see the results, rather than being dead.

For those who allow themselves to be brainwashed, give that a little more thought. For many years, adult men and women have been misled into taking their life and their children's lives because of fanatics who described themselves as the messiah. Wow! You follow a peaceful way of life and then along comes a man who talks you into becoming violent. Come on! You are smarter and better than that.

The world is religious and also scientific. Every one person is not the same and does not think the same way. There are big differences, and there are subtle differences. Sometimes there are no differences. At least 95 percent believe in religion, but that number is declining. Even those who are undecided have the ability to recognize when this fake messiah is filling their head with a load of crap.

It is simple! When someone tells you that you must give up your life by killing others, because of a belief, they have misspoken. The only reason your life becomes in peril is when you are defending it or defending an attack on the peace and tranquility that we all want and are trying to maintain. Contrary to popular belief from terrorists, you are not the only ones who will give up your life just to prove a point. There are countrymen around the world who will give up their lives defending their freedom and peaceful way of life. The only difference is that they will not strap a bomb around their shoulders just to scare people into converting to your religion or believing that they will do anything to get to you.

You can call it a battle of wits, or a game of chess where the result turns out to be the destruction of life as we know it, where someone has to win. This battle is not a game, but if anyone looks at it as such, the only way to win is not to play.

The Bible and Other
Books of Religion

Just a little bit…

FOR SOME PEOPLE, these are simply books, but books that have lasted throughout the ages—books that have significant details that describe man and humanity's creation as we first realized ourselves, right here in the third world. For others, it is the coronet of religion and faith that guides us (spiritually) to this very second. So, where did the Bible come from? Well, it certainly didn't come from someone snapping their fingers and all of a sudden, there it is.

For that small group of people who place scientific correlation with the Bible, they are believers, unsure believers, and disbelievers. One thing for sure though is that they all agree the book is emphatically the oldest book in the world that have been handed down through the generations. Also, they believe that it gives some but not all accurate accounts of history and how it affects us today.

Those who don't believe should not be judged because of their knowledge and the way they were brought up from childhood. Christians, Jews, Protestants, Muslims, or any other religion, have no right to pass judgment on people because they simply say they don't believe. However, the same people may or may not have been exposed to the languages that were handed down for centuries, and are still being translated today.

These books were written by men who witnessed events in the past and recorded them on paper or some form of document that imprinted the language of that time. Through the decades, that language was interpreted to clear text for all nationalities to see. From the very beginning, it describes not the big bang theory of evolution, but the creation of the world that was empty but yet had the possibility to flourish life. When you think about it, Earth was unlivable in the beginning. Life as we know it today could not have possibly survived the intense bombardment, radiation, heat, poisonous gasses, and pressures that were a part of the earth's birth and atmosphere during that time. The earth was born and growing, just like a fetus, in a woman's womb. It needed time to mature and develop into a place of inviolability. This work of art was written in the Bible but to a small extent. Let's talk about that for a few minutes.

Imagine the very first words, in the Bible where it reads, "In the beginning." We all know that according to the dictionary and all conscious thought that "In the beginning" refers to the first—not the middle and not the last, but the **FIRST**. Certainly, if the Bible had started off with "In the middle," we would have to wonder: what happened to the beginning? Well, simply said, "In the beginning" is certainly where it all began, and for some, it is the answer to where it will all end.

Now let us look at the world from a different perspective. What I mean is to imagine that you were holding a twelve-inch by twelve-inch transparent box in your hand. You look at it and see that within it is a swirling mass of darkness and gasses. What's making this mass swirl is not the fact that you are holding it in your hand but that something is pulling against something. **What that something is will be discussed a little later.** However, you see nothing else there. No formed objects, no solid shapes, nothing. Why is that? Let's say it's because you haven't put anything in there. So, who, or what does that make you?

Well, it would seem that since you are holding the box, you are God, according to the beliefs of all generations. You are bigger than any imagination, you are bigger than vision, and you are immeasurable. You are a force so strong that you cannot be seen. Yet, some humans have a perception that you can be felt. To take it further, you can do anything that you want so you decide to take this swirling mass of darkness and gasses and allow it to condense. The gasses gets small, smaller, and smallest until they gather so much energy they explode. The energy begins to expand and take up every bit of room you have in that transparent box. What do you do now, because your energy within that box is demanding more space?

Well, you are God, so you increase the size of that box and fill it with dark matter. This dark matter is absorbing that expanding energy, but controlling how fast it grows, and yet this same energy is demanding more space. Now you form a substance that develops deep inside this energy of darkness and masses where violent collisions of rocks, boulders, and extremely explosive combinations of chemicals produce even more scalding hot energy. You allow millions and millions of parts of this energy to unite, and over a period you decide to cool some of it off.

In the center, you place a ball of hot, solid energy that is known today as the sun. It throws part of its photonic rays out in all directions. It floats and reacts to a force known as gravity as it pulls rocks, boulders, and debris toward it. But those objects seem to have energy of their own. They compete until they come into a steady, flowing circle that leaves a relatively safe distance between each of them. That took a long time.

Now, when you look at what you have just made, you allow the people of today to believe that you put life on one of those rocks. You ask yourself, "Which one would I put an image of myself on?" You look at all of the rocks and decide on the third one from that big scalding hot object. You make it possible for microscopic life to develop first, and then realize that you want complex life to flourish. You see that it is fitting and capable of multiplication and advancement. However, you're not quite ready to make that happen yet. You allow an atmosphere that is breathable that gives a climate that changes from warm to cool, hot to cold, and an atmosphere that adjusts and change to the activities around it. This activity is that massive energy in your box that continues to grow, and yet it moves at millions of miles per hour, and some at millions of miles per second. **This rapid motion of energy is an equation of time that we will talk about later.**

On the side that your photonic rays are touching, and millions of years later, your third world lights up and displays a beautiful blue sky, covered with scattered clouds that look like cotton balls constantly changing shape. It's warm with no futuristic odors. On the side where the photonic rays are not touching, the sky is dark, cool and clear. It displays a beautiful sky filled with twinkling stars and portraying a haze that seems to be endless. From moment to moment, shooting stars' zip across the sky, indicating continuous activity beyond the third world.

Now is the point where you decide to place a single entity on that third world and form it into the image of yourself. You pick out a location with fruits and water because this entity will be organic and made from carbon compounds, which is gathered space dust. It will need nourishment, food, and water. It will be your proudest moment and is indeed the first; It is the beginning.

As the third world swoops around the sun and stays in tune with those other rocks, the light becomes night. As it continues its motion, it turns around, and the light becomes day. The life form that you placed in your image, you now call "man." You give him a name, and that name is Adam. He is the first human being. He is one of the most complex organic compounds ever created. He is living, breathing, thinking, talking, and is in the flesh with an eternal lifespan.

Adam was not perfect and was vulnerable in every way. He became lonely, so you gave him a companion, which you pulled from his rib. That companion had the same appearance, but with a different anatomical structure. That companion was also weak, just like Adam, and some would go as far to say even weaker. Shortly afterward, they performed a single activity that angered you and caused you to start the process of aging. Now life in the flesh is no longer forever. Time is ticking, and the clock continues to count to this day.

What we have just discussed is typically the way people believe and an idea of what they think God is and the image of his likeness. The truth is, as far as we know, no one has seen him and when that time comes our wildest imaginations will be realized, and the person holding the box will appear. The bottom line is that the majority of people believe that God is real and that he has prepared a place of magnificent glory where everything we see, everything we feel, and everything we do is without blemish or darkness. The light will forever shine, and a smile will be imprinted on our spiritual being. Do you believe this? Why do you, and if you don't, why not?

GOD AND SPACE...

As it stands now, and what we are made to believe, is that our scientists and governments have not found any identifiable life within our nine or ten planetary system. Is this because God wants us to be alone or is it because we just don't recognize what life looks like? To step beyond the knowledge that we possess in recognizing what is real or not is a hard thing to do. Could we be standing next to something that is alive and our human comprehension doesn't see that? Certainly, from the probes that are flying through the darkness of outer space, that difficulty remains. However, in the Bible, there is evidence that something was seen and not recognized as human by the people of that day. These somethings are moving, stopping, staring, talking, and flying with or without noise. What are they? Where do they come from and what do they want? Some people refer to them as angels. Science refers to them as irregularities. On the other hand, our scientists and governments are not being completely honest with us on what information they do have pertaining to life beyond the third world.

The Bible speaks a lot about angels. This Bible is indeed the interpretation of the people of that day. Keep in mind that these people did not have the knowledge of today. Their interpretation of an object or something is limited to their understanding and beliefs, and their description could be considered flawed by not only scientist, but any person of today. I mean, if you had the knowledge of today and went back in time to the Bible days, would you call those sightings the same thing that those people of that day did? You probably would or you probably wouldn't. It depends on how strong your faith is.

Some scientists who spend the majority of their time trying to disprove the Bible and put in that piece of the puzzle called evolution agree that angels are real, but they also believe that they may be a mistaken interpretation of a dream or a visitation from a life form that was not familiar to the people of that day. Some scientists may refer to those people as "time travelers." Either way, the Bible is indeed a book that has answers to some questions about the world, where it came from, how it started, what we can do with it, its vulnerability, and how it's going to end. It also gives information on the capability of men and women and how they think and respond to changes, changes that require rapid thinking. However, even today, people tend to respond very slowly. This slow response is why it is important for every leader of a nation to read and understand the oldest book in the world. It is not necessarily all about religions but a window in time and a step into the future. It is history with answers. It gives us the knowledge to advance far beyond the third world.

JESUS CHRIST...

Now, let us talk briefly about this man called Jesus Christ. After all, according to the Bible, he is the way, the truth, and the life, and for those who believe in that, through him is the only way that they will have a spiritual and flawless everlasting life. Is he the one holding the box? Did he bring himself down to the third world to teach and make people believe that indeed there is a place to go after the flesh has ceased to function? This term, "cease to function," is called death; it is the termination of all mortal function of life. Well, what exactly is this? It may even have something to do with time and dimensions. **We will talk about this too a little later as we explore dying and death.**

According to the Bible, Jesus Christ arrived through the womb of a woman who had no physical contact by the normal way that we all are accustomed. He grew up as a normal child, but with strange abilities that made him stand out—abilities that no one else had. Even with these capabilities, he too was vulnerable, and that is because he was meant to feel the feelings that children felt. He was meant to grow up as a man and walk through the agony, pain, and disappointments that are sometimes unavoidable. According to the Bible, he was also meant to die.

So, this man who could do things that nobody else could do was the nicest man that the world who knew him ever new. He never mocked anyone, and he certainly didn't lie about a thing. But he performed many miracles—even bringing the dead back to life. Was he a magician that had the upper edge, or was he originally the true and one and only Trinity?

Theologians and some scientist will go as far to say that he is "The Christ." Others say that he was a magician because they compared some of the things he did back then to today. Magicians can perform incredible eye-opening and seemingly impossible feats that are seen on television today. What they can't prove is that he brought the dead back to life, and in fact he came back to life after three days of being dead. He also fed a multitude with a hand full of food. That's a lot of people with just a small amount of bread.

Now this is an interesting concept, because the magicians of today have not been able to replicate all of the miracles that Jesus did. Scientists articulate that doctors can bring people back to life after being dead, so what is the difference? They also say that babies can be born without sexual contact and the possibility of that being the case in the Bible days does exist. However, the problem is proving it.

Well, doctors can bring people back to life after death, but the truth is, those people have only been dead for a brief moment; not three days, and certainly not in the fictional Frankenstein way. For someone to wake up after three days, they should have some amnesia and weakness. Therefore, they probably were not dead but in a comatose state. However, this is only a guess.

When Jesus woke up, was he groggy, weak, and with amnesia? The truth is, we weren't there, and we have to go on what the people who were there had to say about it. This acitivity is what you call history.

Once again, the people in the Bible days were not scholars with a wealth of knowledge, and their interpretation could be flawed based on their understanding during that period. However, the question remains about how babies were conceived during the Bible days, and is that any different from how babies are conceived today?

We all agree that babies are conceived without physical contact the normal way that we are accustomed. That is because of test-tube technology. Did they have that in the Bible days? We weren't there, and I can't find it in the Bible; so, since it wasn't mentioned, it doesn't mean that it didn't happen. Therefore, for now, we have to go off of Immaculate Conception, because we have no proof of any other way, and we have no proof of Immaculate Conception. However, it does bring up a very good question: are we alone, in this massive quantity of infinite space? The truth will be known, and it will be known soon. So why talk about the Bible in the beginning portion of this book? Because it has complex answers that are useful to the technology of today. Sometimes, reading between the lines is a good thing. Are our leaders doing that?

World leaders must understand the concept of the Bible and the message that it offers us. Since man wrote it, it may not be 100 percent accurate, but the messages are not to be ignored. There are problems in this world, and there are problems outside of this world. Ultimately, these problems will merge and could present as a global threat. This merge may be a time for leaders and clergy to read between the lines and work together.

It is obvious that the message was ignored, and that seems to emanate from the beginning. Some ask what it will take for leaders to take action. Some are listening, but are they understanding? Most importantly, do they have the means to fix the problem? The answer is obviously a yes. However, the human heart is weak, hard, and stubborn. Each moment in time that nothing is done, people (and I mean good people) die. This problem can be prevented simply by understanding the magnitude of ignoring signs and taking actions. Actions include divulging information that may be helpful to the world's population, regardless of what some leaders believe the truth may cause.

We have books with messages. We have to read it. In a sense, it is still being written. It's just a matter of placing the puzzle altogether. Once you do this, the picture will be complete. Then lives **WILL** be saved. On the other hand, is there anything else that can be done? We have people who are devout believers; will they follow the word of these books completely? It does bring up an interesting question.

In the Bible, there are the Ten Commandments. Will those who believe in the Ten Commandments try to adhere to them 100 percent?

Let's see…

Commandment number one: "I am the lord your God. You shall have no other Gods besides me."

With all of the religious books in the world and the many false leaders who write about and talk about themselves being God or a messenger of God, and lead you to commit crimes and take your life, doesn't this violate the first commandment?

Commandment number two: "You shall not make for yourself a carved image or any likeness of anything that is in heaven above, or that is in the earth beneath, or that is in the water under the earth; you shall not bow down to them nor serve them. For I, the Lord your God, am a jealous God, visiting the iniquity of the fathers on the children to the third and fourth generations of those who hate me, but showing mercy to thousands, to those who love me and keep my Commandments."

There are carved images, statues, and other erections around the world. Some people worship them, and some don't. This behavior is a choice that some people are going to hate. It is a natural occurrence of humanity and it is something that we must try to control. What that means is that everybody doesn't like everybody. Moreover, the second commandment mentions that God is jealous. Truly, those who believe say that God is greater than anything or anyone. So, why would God be jealous when he is the ultimate, and no one or nothing can match or step beyond his magnificence? It doesn't mean you have to disbelieve; you simply want to understand.

The second commandment also mentions that we should not murder. Well, maybe some people don't quite understand what murdering is. Let me elaborate.

When you take someone's life, either by shooting, stabbing, beating, choking, hanging, or decapitating his or her head, and those people do not desire that, or anything like it to happen to them, that is murder. If you believe in any of these books that direct your life, then you will follow what is written. What is troublesome is that some books allow for killings of innocent people, although some have a flawed interpretation of what innocence is.

In the Bible, there is a passage in Deuteronomy that came from Jesus. It instructs believers to stone, until death, those who worship other Gods or don't believe in the way of his teachings. That's murder! So, what happened to "You shall not murder?"

Other books describe the same thing. It's particularly identified in Israel, Iraq, and those countries where the readings are followed, regardless of the value of life. Remember, when you take a life, you take away the world's future.

What does it take to save lives? What is this other thing? Will it take something as simple as making a choice? Or does it take money? If so, how much will that be? Since the monetary system has to stay, although we have the capability to do without it, we should make the best of it as it pertains to saving humanity and all life that flourishes on the third world. So how much money can each country afford to give to save the world?

Understanding the US Budget and the World's Financial Summary

THE PURPOSE OF this description is to establish cause and ability and see why deceit seems to be a major factor with decision-makers. The purpose is also to understand the value and capability to plan and proceed without reservations and to give a researched explanation as to why progress is slow and why trickery, ignorance, and selfishness prevail. One question that should be asked is can the world survive without money? We shall begin with the United States of America.

Once affirmed as the most powerful country in the world, America seems to be loosening on its grace and charm. It is mainly due to the ability of this nation to respond to threats and the fact that they have a nuclear arsenal that is unmatched by any other country. Or so we think. This ability is indeed power, but a kind of power that displays might, stamina, grit, and pushiness. Where are the kindliness and human love that the United States was once known for?

Where is that handshake that meant friendship and care, not lies and disregard for the preservation of life and the future of humanity?

It wasn't always this way, but the older you get, it seems the more deceitful and cheaper you get. I am not referring to every member of Congress, Governor, Mayor or member of the federal decision-makers, because most of them are honest and caring folks. I am referring to those few who have the power to cast a vote that sometimes outnumber the good guys. How did they get there? Well, we put them there.

These politicians are referred to as greedy and do not believe that there are agendas more important than their own. They are a part of democracy that has existed for many years. They have a priority that is not in agreement with the concerns of the people. They work for all levels of government: the executive, legislative and judicial.

Yes, our level of democracy has taken the best of us because we have the power to make a difference, whether good or bad. This debacle is a problem, and it must be addressed. The question is how? And how do we tackle the "I got mine, he got his, but we don't have ours" syndrome? It's a major task but let's give it a try! First, let's see how much money the United States is believed to have.

The United States has paper currency and coins in petty cash that are somewhere in the neighborhood of $300 billion. Not much for a country that sports the greatest military fighting force in the world, and claims to be one of the richest. Certainly, the military is not cheap! However, this is just a small portion, as an economist has dictated that the spending amount is about $900 billion, and the savings amount exceeds $5 trillion. This part is just the inclusive statement of the money supply with the savings account included. In other words, the currency plus deposit into checking equals the money that is spent. So where does the United States get the money that it boasts about in all its richness? The truth is that the United States is not broke. If you were to put a country in a neighborhood, the United States would live in Beverly Hills.

The United States borrows money and make it. That's right! The United States is borrowing money from banks from around the world with no intent to pay it back; at least, that is the impression that it is giving. Also, it is physically making the money (not bootleg, mad dog counterfeiting) because the Treasury Department prints it. However, let's say that it does pay some of it back in currency, which makes for just 1 percent of the complete worth. Well, if they pay in wire transfers between banks, they are paying less than 0.2 percent, maybe 59 percent of the dollars (rough estimates).

So, what does this mean?

Simply put, the government is not making money appear out of thin air. If you look at it closely, you will see that private banks are doing that, and it's by the skin of each American, or visitor who pays taxes, and who deposits money into their private American bank account. The banks invest that money in hopes that you wouldn't take it out right away. The more money you deposit, the more money the banks can lend to the guy in the red, white, and blue top hat, and since there are supposedly 308,442,650 people, give or take visitors, and new citizens in the United States, how come the United States is in debt? Yes, during presidential campaigns, it has been mentioned that the United States is in debt. Is that the truth? Or does debt mean something else?

If each one of these 308 plus million people gave $5, imagine how much money that would equal. Moreover, if each one of these people gave $10, the amount of money that sits in the bank is enough to last forever, especially when each year brings a percentage of interest. It would seem that there is ample amount of money to provide for health care, research, building spacecraft's, protecting the earth, and feeding the hungry—especially since the amount taxed exceeds an average of more than $500 per low-income person.

Some other ways that the federal government makes money is the same way that cities make money. It obtains it by selling bonds. Then, it pays off the bonds by selling newer bonds. The interest generated is like the US Mint itself, where the money made enhances the owner and makes them rich—that owner being the President of the United States for the people with the capability to dip into the US Federal Reserve System, which (by the way) is unaccountable to no one.

Selling land and property is another way as well as making the sovereign Indian nation pay for the ability to operate on their land. You know—the lands our ancestors took forcibly, felt bad about it, and gave back. These Indians are nice about it because they see that the economy is in a slump, and so they step up to the plate and give what they believe is right. They also help not only the Indian land people but communities, groups, hospitals, and other entities through gifts, sponsorship, and grants. Oh, of course, the United States is doing the same and on a larger perspective, but deceit remains. Is this deceit also part of paying taxes?

Your taxes/my taxes

Taxes! Taxes! Taxes! We are all taxed every time we bring in a paycheck or make over a certain amount of money. We are also taxed every time we go to the store and buy something. Sometimes that amount is over $1,199, and sometimes you get taxed after making just 21 cents. Depending on your dependent claims and whether you itemize, you may be paying 9 cents of those 21 cents. Are there some people who are not taxed on anything? Yep, there sure are, but I will get into that a little later. For now, let me murmur the words of many people who believe they should not pay taxes, "Like hell, I will give my hard-earned money to the state or federal government to cheat and make crooked deals without my permission!" Some of these people believe they have the right not to pay taxes, and most of them are spending time next to a great big man or woman who stares at them every night as they sit in a small, weird-shaped cell called PRISON. Some others find that their paycheck is garnished, their property has a lean on it, and/or their credit is negatively affected. Nonetheless, this is where our money is going, and that is to the government.

When you give your hard-earned money to the state or federal government, that money is supposed to be used for the benefit of the people. Let's look at that and see just how much money one average person gives—but before that, let's take a look at the other countries around the world, and how they can contribute from their financial standpoint.

World finance has a lot to do with government. Although there are many billionaires and millionaires, the government seems always to have a hold of their money in some way. That money is in direct correlation to what and how the United States puts its money to work. They support their respected countries from the military to medical, to legal to space programs. The space programs are not in every country, but the ones who have it have a pretty massive budget, and yet it's not enough to do an adequate function of discovery, protection, and exploration.

If one were to add up the world's finances by the working people of individual countries (some 4.170 billion), annually the gross worth would be around $70 trillion. When you factor in the businesses (not governments), of which there are some 200 million (including small and new businesses), the gross worth could be around $900 trillion x2. Now, we want to factor in the gross worth of each government. Mind you that each administration has the aptitude to make their money, not by taxes but by print. Therefore, the actual amount is insignificant. However, let's give it a number, or a name, say like trillions and trillions and trillions of dollars. This money is crazy!

With all this scattered money around the world, why in the hell are there homeless people and dying people that are unable to reach health care—including veterans—welfare, and poor dental accessibilities after a $1,000 or $2,000 deductible? But most importantly, in my opinion, why are we not depositing more money into medical research and the understanding of ourselves and our home world?

Nothing is permanent! So why don't we use some of this crazy money to find out what to do when the earth is threatened with destruction or extinction of all life as we know it? It's time to act. We are simply a vessel traveling through time and space and as with anything that is traveling, it MUST come to an end. What does that mean? It means that something will stop us either by fragmentation, incineration, being frozen solid, or the stripping of our atmosphere, which can happen rapidly and quietly. Basically, the termination of human life is approaching, and our leaders have it placed on the back burner where they may or may not get to it at some unimportant point of their time. Can they do something about it? In my opinion, YES, THEY CAN. The question is, will they?

If any humans stepped outside of his or her domain and just look around, what would he or she see? Or better yet, what would he or she experience? The experience would be beauty, tranquility, quietness, fresh air, and a soothing, smooth summer, winter, spring, and fall breeze that gives a feeling of freedom and safety. However, this is a temporary situation, and it is NOT like that in some other places. It's hell that no one should ever have to endure.

What the hell is hell?

In the Old Testament of the King James version of the Bible, the word hell is mentioned thirty-one times, and in the New Testament, it is mentioned twenty-three times for a total of fifty-four times. What exactly does this mean? Well, looking around the world where trouble is in abundance, hell could be a place of burning torment, suffering from no end, or a torrential downfall of terminal emotional grief. Further in the Bible, hell is referred to as the deepest abyss, prison, the grave, or the "dead." Nonetheless, hell seems to be an unpleasant place to be. So, why has it existed for many years and is going strong today? Am I referring to hell above the earth, where people flourish? Or am I referring to hell where some people typically believe to exist, which is below Earth? Certainly, I am referring to where the animate people are.

Greed is the reason for many aspects of trouble. Everywhere around the world, it takes currency for people to get what they need for the basic elements of survival. Why is it so hard for this to happen? It is because the people who can make a difference are not listening. Their agenda is not wholly on the needs of the people of the world but their personal want.

This is hell...

In Afghanistan, since 2001 to now, over 28,000 people, including civilians and military, have been violently and viciously killed. The types of deaths include explosions, gunshots, stabbings, beheadings, rapes, stoning's, decapitation, incinerations, and beatings.

Looking further back in Afghanistan's recent history, not much has changed. These are people who live and breathe. They desire the essentials for life. The reason they are fighting has a lot to do with their beliefs, values, and an unknown agenda. Their enemy is not only the forces they are fighting, but perhaps, themselves. They are human beings, and they want to live. Can they be left alone and live a life of peace and harmony?

The people who can answer this question are you and I. We must determine the reason for fighting and find a medium to discuss it. With our combined knowledge of human understanding, the outcome could be remarkably favorable. We just have to give ourselves the chance to do it. It is about time that we use our inner functions of mental reality and interpretation. If we cannot do this, our future is grim, which means the human race and all life on this planet is at risk of extinction.

As you can see, we have come a long way since our first understanding of time and existence. We are advancing. Our brains are getting smarter, and each time a child is born, a new advance technology begins to grow. If we eliminate life, we eliminate technology, and we will need it in the years to come. So, the world's budget and financial future depend on each and every one of us, from all nationalities and all countries. The financial budget is the financial budget of life.

The World's Military

AS IT STANDS right now, not every nation has a military force. Some are very powerful, some mediocre, and some are just in a category of a local police force. Nonetheless, each nation has the capability to defend against aggression. However, the strength of a military force is in its leadership, equipment, discipline, technology, and respect. The personnel who are members of these military forces display a quality of respect that will ultimately result in victory. Let's take a look at the leadership.

The mark of a leader does not always depend on the leader's knowledge and educational levels. It has a lot to do with traits, upbringing, and values. Therefore, a question that should be asked about leadership is what kind of leader will lead troops into victory, and ultimately achieve a goal? Is it the dictator type, such as the one whose agenda centers on just one thing: himself? Or is it the kind that takes advantage of all of his or her resources and then makes a decision to achieve a goal?

These are the types that (for the most part) achieved victory, but seemingly, temporarily. They include Napoleon Bonaparte, Fidel Castro, Khadafy, and Hitler. These leaders had traits that were no match against the leaders to whom they were battling against. However, because of those traits, their decisions during battle turned out to be flawed. On the other hand, these leaders were brilliant, regarding leading their nation and their troops. The way they communicated displayed a type of path-goal leadership that allowed them to achieve the position that they were currently in. Their militaries might have demonstrated all levels of technology and planning. Each one had an arsenal that had the capability to destroy entire continents. However, it wasn't until the latter years of World War II that demonstrated a lethal and global threat. It was nuclear and was first tested and used by the United States of America.

It wasn't until four years later when the Soviet Union decided to dabble with nuclear weapons and participate in their test. They were successful, and their egos elevated beyond belief. Shortly after that, the United Kingdom and China realized that they were being left behind in this new terminology called the nuclear race. They too tested nuclear weapons by detonation and became part of this worldwide, massively flexed bicep muscle.

Realizing the destructive potential of these weapons, some states decided to create the Nuclear Nonproliferation Treaty (NPT), because they felt that some states shouldn't be allowed to have them. Although many signatures were gathered from country leaders, most were not, and the testing and detonation of nuclear weapons continued. Some of those states include Pakistan, Israel, and even India. Someone may wonder: how can these latter countries afford to put together such a lethal arsenal? Well, the answer is easy: they're rich because big nations like the United States, Japan, United Kingdom, the Soviet Union, and other countries pay them for their oil and other precious materials. Furthermore, you really can't tell another country what to do with their technology because if you even tried to, most of their leaders will tell you to shove it where the sun doesn't shine.

Currently, a limited retaliation of arms is used by a nation that attacked another nation. The nuclear aspects have been disciplined, and if used, a huge price will be paid. Conventional weapons are preferred and allow for a lesser range of lasting destruction. Let us not forget the ultimate power of just one nuclear bomb. Today, nuclear weapons are more powerful and have the potential to bring an end to humanity as we know it. Let us look at six nations' military power and discuss what they have to offer.

THE UNITED STATES OF AMERICA

—Defense budget is just over $600,000,000

AFTER THE END of the Vietnam War, the United States continued to build its military might and portray itself in first place as the most powerful military in the world. However, with each newly elected President, that first-place standing appeared to be questionable, because Congress and other politicians wanted to save money. Fortunately, other countries were no match in comparison to the United States because of money, and their military might be smaller.

The flexed arm of the Eagle indicates over 1.4 million active-duty military personnel and nearly 900,000 reserve personnel. There are well over 130 million personnel who are fit for service and just under 5 million who are reaching the military fighting age. There are close to 9,000 tanks, nearly 14,000 aircraft including fighter jets, attack helicopters, trainer aircraft, fixed-wing attack aircraft, transports, and drones. The US has well over 42,000-armed fighting vehicles, 13,000 towed artillery, 20,000 self-propelled guns, and 14,000 multiple-launch systems. There are an untold number of special operation units that can appear and disappear with the snap of a finger. These are expert combat personnel who react when the command is given. Their mission has a nearly 100 percent success rate, so when an enemy is targeted, the time to say good-bye would be then and now. Advance technology includes drones and laser capability.

The United States Navy sports a compared strength of over 416,000 personnel with 11 mine warfare ships, 19 aircraft carriers, 7 frigates, over 62 destroyers, about 14 coastal defense crafts, and over 75 submarines. Her technology as compared to wars past has surpassed the thought of science fiction and replaced it with science fact. Anyone who dares to test the attack capability, preparation, technology, readiness, and swiftness of the United States military should think twice because the moment you attempt to knock that stick off the shoulder of the Eagle, your life function will cease before that stick hits the ground.

As you are probably aware, the United States military has scientists on active duty, in the reserves, and under contract. Experiments and discoveries are not always disclosed for good reason, and national security tops the list. Others include patency, or that most tests need to be evaluated further. Scientists work every day to find ways for ground troops to survive, for aircraft to keep flying if struck by a missile, and to target the enemy with pinpoint accuracy from thousands of miles away. What would be interesting is how the pilot will make it safely to friendly territory.

The United States also depends on oil production, but is slowly phasing that necessity out. Some believe that the military can operate most of its equipment without the eight million oil production barrels per day. With that, the entire country consumes over twenty million barrels per day. The United States is considered a powerful nation.

THE REPUBLIC OF CHINA

—Defense budget is $220,000,000

CHINA HAS DEMONSTRATED that it too is extremely intelligent and on a constant basis is building its military to a powerful force. China's technology parallels the United States as their scientists develop and place into use ground, air, and space-base technology that will protect them from any aggressor. There is special forces who train rigorously in cold and intemperate weather. Of course, all military members from military nations do this, but China lives in it almost on a constant basis.

The flexed arm of the dragon indicates an over 755,000,000 military personnel with 625,000,000 that are ready to fight. On top of that, there are well over 21,000,000 who are about to be eligible for military services. There are over 6,000,000 active and reserve personnel who are in shape, educated, and in a position to strike if the order is given.

China's military is battle ready with over 10,000 tanks, 6,500 armored towed artillery, a little less than 1,800 multiple launch rocket systems, 1,800 self-propelled guns, and less than 5,000-armed fighting vehicles. Moreover, her naval arsenal sports 720 ships, currently 1 aircraft carrier, 50 frigates, 35 destroyers, 69 active and ready submarines, 140 coastal-defense crafts, and three mine-warfare ships.

The Air Force of China sports over 3,000 overall aircraft, 785 transport aircraft, about 140 attacks and fixed wing aircraft, and 812 attack helicopters. Furthermore, China depends on oil as well, but that, just like in the United States, is changing. China is also very respectful of traditions and traits.

In my years of serving in the military, I have encountered Chinese troops. My first impression is that they are well trained and follow a strict military code of justice. They are friendly and speak with direct eye contact, hand shaking and bowing. I can't help but think that most of this behavior came from their upbringing from parents and relatives who taught respect for rank, the person, and the country.

China also has special forces who can appear and disappear at the snap of a finger. To test China's military is like walking through a pit of black mambas. You simply would wish you hadn't. Moreover, China continues to build both on land and underground. Underground is smart and gives an extreme advantage to secrecy, which protects China's national security. Perhaps these underground bases allow for military planes, spaceships, and submarines to come in, park, do some cool experiments, and leave. Satellites can see them in the water but not through solid granite and rock. China is considered a powerful nation.

RUSSIA

—Defense budget is $85,000,000,000

CURRENTLY KNOWN AS the largest country in the world, Russia's gross domestic product is 2.097 trillion US dollars. It is probably three percent of the world's economy. Russia's military is extremely powerful, as they sport a space program, just like China, Japan, the United States, and a few others, and their technology is keen with excellent scientists who are in the military and are civilians.

The flexed arm of the double-headed eagle indicates an active and reserve frontline force of over 100,000,000 personnel. There are just over 48,000,000 who are ready should the call go out. There are 1,400,000 personnel who are on the cusp of legally joining the military. Russia's might include a tank force of just over 15,000, multiple-launch rocket systems of about 4,000, self-propelled guns at 6,000, 32,000 armored fighting vehicles, and towed artillery of about 5,000.

Russia's superior air power dominates the skies with about 3,600 aircraft, 480 attack helicopters, 1,300 regular helicopters, about 1,500 attack fixed-wing aircraft, and topping off with 749 fighter aircraft. Russia's special forces are well equipped, prepared, and in shape as they train in virtually every terrain. Just like the United States, Russia sports snipers and military personnel with special skills to fit any mission.

Russia's naval forces dog the waters with over 350 ships, 59 submarines, and one aircraft carrier—but who's to say more are not in progress. She sports 15 destroyers and 4 or 5 fast frigates. There are 15 coastal-defense crafts, and she may be putting a squadron of drones together for unmanned missions.

Russia is a mighty force with leaders who have experience, education, wit, and patience. It is clear that her president is in control, which shows a well-organized nation of people that display extreme respect and dedication. If an aggressor thinks about challenging the Russian military, the retaliation would be untold with destructive consequences. Russia is considered to be a powerful nation.

JAPAN

—Defense budget is $41,500,000,000

JAPAN IS ANOTHER one of those countries that has people who respect other people's traditions and beliefs. It has been many decades since the attack on Pearl Harbor, and since her military was reduced to a local police force. Today, Japan demands the respect of the world because it has worked hard to rebuild its image and military might. We know that war is hell, but we must understand that it is in the past and lessons have been learned. The United States and Japan share a friendship that is binding and unbreakable. Quite possibly, if we should go back in time many years before Pearl Harbor and look at the reasons for the attack, abstract thought would have intervened and it would never have happened—although, information in those days was limited to communication with a typewriter.

Like a bobcat, Japan flexes its muscles with an active and reserve force of over 300,000 personnel. There are just fewer than 46,000 others who are fit for military duty. Coming close to the required age to enter the military are 1,250,000 people. These are strong, dedicated, and respectful people. To add to Japan's might are 670 tanks, over 2,700 armored fighting vehicles, about 101 multi-launch vehicles, just under 500 towed artillery, and 200 self-propelled guns.

Japan controls the air with over 1,500 aircraft, just under 290 fighter aircraft, under 300 fixed-wing attack aircraft, 640 helicopters, and 120 attack helicopters. The forces are strong with the latest technology and nearly daily training activity. Japan's air power is superior, but her navy is equally destructive.

Japan naval forces sports a total of 3 aircraft carriers, 44 destroyers, 16 submarines, five coaster defense crafts, and 27 mine warfare ships. Japan's knowledge of the sea is superior and dates back to ancient Japan. Moreover, the total population of the country is well over 127,000,000 people.

I have had the pleasure of working with one of my closest friends as he became a paramedic in California. His attitude and personality were amazingly kind. He smiled frequently and was eager to learn new ways of treating emergency patients. Unfortunately, his papers expired, and he had to return to Japan. I have maintained communication with him.

My friend is a shining example of all of the people of Japan. They are kind, friendly, and care about the people they meet and the ones around them. In particular, I am impressed with their prostration and etymology. The words spoken are fast and seem slurred, but impressive at the same time. Japan is considered a powerful nation

INDIA

—Defense budget is $45,000,000,000

THE TIGER IS a powerful and engaging animal. What makes the Tiger so fearsome is that it is patient, swift, and commands a voice that is heard throughout the land. India's military is the same way. It is formidable and fearless and will take on an enemy, regardless of how powerful they are. The military force has an active and reserve strength of over 3,500,000, with an available manpower force of over 600,000,000 with 490,000,000 fit for duty. The force about to reach enlistment age reaches 24,000,000. India is no pushover. Their forces include special operations units that are quick to respond with lethal and pinpoint accuracy.

India's military force contains about 7,000 tanks, 7,000 armored fighting vehicles, 290 multiple-launch vehicles, over 7,000 towed artillery, and 285 self-propelled guns. Her air power includes a total of over 2,000 aircraft, 18 attack helicopters, 640 regular helicopters, 681 fighters, and over 800 fixed-wing aircraft. Her naval force is also formidable, with 2 aircraft carriers, 13 frigates, 11 destroyers, 13 submarines, 136 coastal-defense crafts, and 5 mine warfare ships.

India is not talked about much in the media. Even with a powerful military force, keeping private seems to be its pastime. However, challenge India and you will face the full brunt of the Tiger's teeth. It would not be pleasant. Furthermore, India, like other nations, will fight until the last soldier is standing. Moreover, for all powerful nations, retreat is not an option. India is considered a powerful nation.

THE UNITED KINGDOM

—Defense budget is $61,000,000,000

THE UNITED KINGDOM descends from a history of royalty. Her greatest gift is the royal family, which began in ancient times and today maintains a high respect from the citizens of the United Kingdom and around the world. They are proud people with a high regard of respect for everyone in every country. Their gross domestic product is 2.7 trillion US dollars with a population of just over 64,000,000 people.

The United Kingdom's royal coat of arms portrays a powerful presence with almost 150,000 active military personnel and about 184,000 reserve personnel. Each year, her citizens reaching the age to serve range from 748,000 to 751,000. It has 407 tanks, 139 towed artillery, 43 multi-launch rocket systems, 88 self-propelled guns, and close to 6,000 armored fighting vehicles.

The United Kingdom's airpower is supreme with the latest technology. It sports a total of 880 aircraft, with 92 being fighters and 169 fixed-wing attack aircraft. It has a total helicopter force of 412. But, what of their naval power?

The United Kingdom's navy prowls the oceans with one carrier, 13 frigates, 5 destroyers, 18 coastal-defense crafts, and several mine-warfare ships. An enemy of the United Kingdom should think twice before testing its defense capability. Like the US and other major powers, there are highly trained special forces with the capability to strike with pinpoint accuracy.

Clearly, the world's military power is a formidable force to contest. Just the power of the previously mentioned nations is strong enough to bring an end to a conflict or bring an end to the world. Other nations with great military power are just as strong with a large army, air force, and naval force. Their budget combined is enough to turn many forces into one powerful world force that, if challenged, would produce a rapid conclusion.

Education

IN THE PAST few years, candidates for public office talked about the importance of education and how it should be achieved free of charge. There are skeptics who disagree because their education cost money, and some if it is still owed today. What is worrisome is that some of those skeptics have children who are about to enter college with intentions of achieving postgraduate education. Do those skeptics desire their children to pay for school? If so, where is the money coming from, other than a grant or education loan? Besides, parents pay a majority of their child's education from start to finish. So, what is wrong with going to school for free? I want to share an incident that occurred with me when I was in high school, in 1979.

It was Wilma Hutchins High School, just outside Dallas. When I was in the ninth grade, my grades were not very attractive. However, as I progressed through high school, I realized that grades play an important part in getting into college. Well, I improved my grades, but they were not good enough for me to get a scholarship—you know, the thing that you get that allows you to go to college for free.

Since I didn't get a scholarship, I called two (what I believed to be) reputable universities. A female answered the phone in the admissions department. I told her that I wanted to get a degree from her school. She sounded very excited and said, "We would love for you to attend our school." She asked me if I lived in Texas and I smiled with the biggest grin and replied, "Yes." I could hear typing as our conversation progressed further.

The lady on the phone continued to ask me questions. "What is your mother's highest grade of education?" I told her that she had completed the sixth grade. She further inquired if she had any more education. I replied, "No." There was silence on the phone to the point where I believed that she had hung up, but with a change in her tone, she remained on the phone.

As our conversation progressed, the lady asked another question: "What is your father's highest grade of education?" I replied, "The sixth grade, but he was drafted into the Navy." Again, the air was filled with silence to the point where I inquired as to whether the lady was still on the phone. By the unchanged tone of her voice, my grin slowly diminished to the point of a blank stare.

"Is there something wrong?" I asked. The lady did not answer after several attempts to get her to respond. Then, she asked another question: "Sir, what is your nationality?" I told her that I was African American.

This time, the lady replied quickly. She told me that since my mother and father did not have an education, and because I was African-American, that I would more than likely be unsuccessful in college.

Wow! What a blow! I tried to explain to her that my mom didn't have the same opportunities, as she was growing up and raising kids, but the next thing I heard was that steady buzz that was familiar on the phone. She had hung up, and that was it.

If there are other African Americans or minorities who have

encountered this same form of rejection, can you imagine what this world has missed? Education is the most powerful weapon that any nation can possess. The fact that there are so many people rejected because of their parents' levels of education, or that they are minorities, limits this world in technology, cures for diseases, and perhaps propulsion advancements in space that are unmatched to what we have today.

Man, has not come this far by faith. However, when opportunities are unreachable, we have a tendency to create our opportunities. Some are in the music industry, such as rap, rhythm and blues, jazz and more. We have taken those industries to another level where the world recognizes it because as the world turns, so do the minds of good people. Hence, when minds go to waste or are unused, the people of the world pay the ultimate price for that.

Today, it seems that when parents are uneducated, getting into college is much easier. This easy access to college is a giant step for humanity because those opportunities are present. We need to teach our children the importance of education and the vast choices of occupations at an early age. What about those successful people, actors, and musicians who do not have a college education or graduate degree?

Well! What about them?

Having a college degree does not guarantee anyone riches with a fabulous life in the limelight. However, it does guarantee your ability to advance the world's technology and most importantly stand as a role model for your children. Regardless of how much money people make, education remains at the forefront of human survival.

Dying and Death

THERE ARE THEORIES as to why people fear death. Some of it has to do with what people know about it. For instance, some believe that it is a painful process as one soul separates and crosses over from the flesh into the spirit. Some believe that they will die twice, because of the way they have been raised and taught. They are told that if they have been bad or evil that they will be punished on the other side. They die in the flesh and then again in hell. Once again, this is a personal belief taught from generation to generation.

Some other fears come from what people see on television, movie theaters, and what they hear on the radio. For instance, the old classic films, such as Frankenstein, or Dracula, demonstrate a genre that visualized people turning into horrible monsters. They are creatures in human form who kill. When they take a life, that person on the other end screams and appears to be in agonizing pain and discomfort. These were the black and white films, but with time came technology. That technology is graphics, color, and improved cinematography.

The images of today's films are extraordinary, as the flow of blood, saliva, and the decapitation of body parts gives a real and spectacular image that frightens the moviegoer to the point of total anxiety and sweat. Here, it is obvious that most people see that death is not desirable, and they do not look forward to facing it.

Because of the images from the media, people turn a blind eye to dying and death. Most of them, particularly teenagers, will not give it a second thought until they are much older and faced with the reality that they will die. They understand that the body cannot continue to function like it used to because of a debilitating illness, traumatic event, or simply getting too old. What is it that people feel when faced with this dilemma?

As I progressed through my early career as an EMT and paramedic, I was presented with a variety of emergency situations. Although the vast majority of those were the elderly, there were large numbers of young, children, and babies who also found themselves in similar situations.

In one particular month, back in 1985, around 4:30 p.m., 911 was activated and I responded to a fifty-five-year-old man with chest pain. When I got to his home, his wife of twenty-four years opened the door. I entered and noticed a strong smell of cigarette smoke. He was sitting on his sofa. A can of beer was sitting on his table, in front of him. His eyes were open and glassy. His breathing was brisk as a faint wheeze sounded with every inhalation and exhalation. He looked at me and said, in the form of an answer, "I'm going to die!"

I approached him, with my drug box and oxygen tank. I quickly felt his pulse. It was irregular, pounding, and rapid. His skin was diaphoretic, cool, and pale. I tried to ease his apprehension by indicating that I was there to help. It didn't matter, because he continued to portray the look of doom. I quickly turned on my oxygen and placed the mask over his face, giving him 100 percent. I started an intravenous and put him on the heart monitor. The rhythm indicated

ST segment elevation, just on lead II. It was clear that he was suffering a heart attack, also known as a myocardial infarction.

I yelled for the firefighters to bring in the gurney as I administered nitroglycerin and gave him aspirin. Suddenly, he moaned, and like the swift strike of a lightning bolt, he slouched back against the sofa. His eyes were staring upward as if he was looking at someone. I called out his name and got no response. He was not breathing, nor did he have a pulse. He was now in cardiac arrest, and cardiopulmonary resuscitation (CPR) was started as his wife ran through the front door. She was screaming and crying. She went immediately toward his face and held his head. She kissed him and begged him to wake up.

As we pushed fast and hard on his chest and administered medication to restart his heart, his wife grasped his right hand and squeezed it. I watched as his hand remained motionless. The tears poured down his wife's eyes as she continued to hold on to him, tightly. His heart was in a rhythm that required a shock from our defibrillator and at this time, his wife was peeled away from him like an orange peeled from its skin. I charged the paddles to 200 watts/second and released the energy. I got no response and did it again at 300 watts/second. I still did not get a heartbeat or an organized rhythm. I charged my paddles and released 360 watts/second of energy into the man's chest. There was no response and CPR was continued.

The man was loaded into the ambulance and transported to the hospital where doctors and nursing personnel worked on him for another twenty-five minutes. The result was that the man died. On his face was the appearance of peace, calmness, and freedom. The look of doom was gone, but for his family, it was just beginning.

On another emergency call, I responded to a suburban neighborhood for a shooting. On the radio, the dispatcher indicated that the shooters were still in the area. The dispatcher also described a thirteen-year-old male with a gunshot wound to his abdomen. Based on the fact that the shooter was still in the area, the ambulance staged at a safe distance. While the police department responded, this thirteen-year-old male was facing death, based on the fact that he had a wound to his abdomen, and it was bleeding both internally and externally.

It was apparent that this was a gang-related shooting. I could hear the chatter on the radio identifying the victim and the shooter as members of a gang. Although it felt like the ambulance was sitting idle for quite a while, it was only eight minutes, and that eight minutes felt like eternity. Moments later, the police department cleared the ambulance onto the scene. Once we arrived, we immediately made contact with the shooting victim. It was a thirteen-year-old Hispanic male with a single gunshot wound to his mid abdomen. There was no exit wound. His eyes were open, glassy, and he had the appearance of doom on his face. This point is where not much is done on the scene because placing the patient on the gurney and treating in route to a trauma center was the most appropriate method to save his life.

While in route to the trauma center, the patient began to sweat, profusely, while his breathing increased, and dark red blood dripped from his mouth. I looked at his body and noticed colorful tattoos around the front part of his neck, reaching toward the back. There were tattoos vertically down his back and on both arms. Some resembled that of the devil, in red, and others resembled angels.

I quickly started a large intravenous bag of normal saline and ran it wide open. The young boy looked up at me, and in a soft Hispanic accent, murmured, "Please, don't let me die!" Tears flowed from both eyes, oozing down the sides of his face. I put an oxygen mass on his face and opened the valve to 100 percent.

As we continued to rush this young boy to the hospital, his heart rate increased to well over 200 beats per minute as his breathing slowed to eighteen breaths per minute, then fourteen, then ten, and then eight breaths per minute. Now it was time to breathe for him. By that time, the ambulance had pulled into the driveway of the trauma center, but the young boy's heart stopped, and so did his breathing. CPR was initiated while removal from the ambulance occurred. The young boy, who at one point became a gang member, died.

For the most part, death is a choice. And in most situations, it is not well thought out. The individuals who engage in dangerous, risky activities and die from gunshot wounds probably did not give it much thought. On the other hand, the person who happens to be minding their own business when a stray bullet finds them is a victim of circumstance. Either way, they face death, and some handle it in different ways than others.

The families who deal with the death of a family member engage in a phase of life that every one of us will encounter. We cannot avoid death, but we can take steps to avoid it until our bodies wear out it in a natural way.

To fear death comes from what we know of death. One thing that we must understand is that this body is just a temporary shell that houses the energy of a soul or spirit that will be released when nature's clock runs out. Even more, the pain that we feel when our loved ones depart is that of connection—that connection is where you can talk to him or her, touch him or her, and laugh and cry with him or her. All that will be no more, and so that connection is gone.

We will miss our family members, and that is why we cry. It is not all the time related to dying; it is how we die and when we die. Dying too young is something that we have not accepted. Dying too old is something that we have accepted but still we feel the pain of missing our loved ones.

We must understand that the human body cannot take too much wear and tear. We must understand that the human body cannot take too much destruction from diseases such as cancer, Alzheimer's, and the like. We must be allowed to terminate our life function and shed a body filled with agonizing pain, discomfort, respiratory distress, and a growing financial burden for our families. Just visualizing a loved one's final moments is terrifying but it quickly becomes acceptable, and as time progresses, the tears and moans go away because the suffering is over.

Terminating our lives is a legal ramification that occurs when our bodies have had enough. We have to explain to our families the reasons why it is necessary to let go. The term is called Do Not Resuscitate (DNR). And when we think of death, we think of time. Death is a time in space, dimensions, and heavens. So when our bodies have had enough, allow us to let go; and then you let go.

Leaders and
Their Decisions

One page!

THERE IS NO doubt that some leaders of the world have made decisions that have affected the lives of people everywhere. Looking back in time, we see this through the eyes of Adolf Hitler, General Tomoyuki Yamashita, Heinrich Otto Abetz, Muto Akira, Abul Kalam Azad, Tariq Aziz, and hundreds more. The agony of the people who suffered is a testimony to what this world has produced over thousands of years. It is too bad that it continues today. So, what does it take for a leader to be a good one?

Some would argue that a good leader rises from the ashes and develops over time with special family traits. Some would argue that a good leader is someone who has been trained to recognize the needs of the people and take action toward the good. So, what happens when a leader has both?

When a leader has both, the people recognize it. Many things that he or she does are well thought out and favorable results are shown. A good leader is one who takes the time to listen and then takes action based on what he or she has heard. The action is not always what people want. However, in the long run, it all pays off in the end.

Earth

Three pages!

THE EARTH AND all of the planets are floating and flying through space at enormous speeds. Although our home is seemingly invincible, in all actuality, it is not. Just like everything that starts with a beginning, it must all come to an end. Fortunately, according to some scientists, that end is not quite near, and some leaders around the world believe that we can "dally" and disregard any efforts to protect the earth and her inhabitants. However, the earth is directly in the path of meteors, comets, and even other planets and stars. What's even frightening is that the earth could be in the path of a black hole. We simply haven't applied enough money actually to know for sure.

One thing that we do know is that the earth will come to an end in many ways. Some are so violent that man should escape to other planets just to keep humanity alive. Some scientists approximate that the earth will have an icy demise, but before that, plate tectonics will get harsh and cause massive earthquakes and tsunamis around the globe. What does this mean for humanity? It is quite simple: we're doomed.

Since the planet inhabitants rely on money for everything, then money is in abundance. Don't tell me it's not, because you know better than that. And if you use simple physics, the earth will die, and money is what it will take to study a bigger portion of the sky, study new proportion systems, and force the atom, magnetism, matter, antimatter, gravity, photons, neutrinos, time, space, and dimensions to work for us, in order to save humanity. It won't take just a little money, but quite a bit. So, if you want to save the earth and be prepared to handle a threat from outer space, being stingy and procrastinating is not the answer.

Is there life on other planets?

Some people say that there is life on other planets and that aliens have visited the earth. Some say that aliens have abducted people. And there are some who say that life does not exist on another planet because there's no mention of it in the Bible. What do we have to say about that?

Well, our eyes can see what appears in front of us. We see colors and turn them into images and objects. Our ears can hear only that which we are accustomed to, and our imagination can conceive and build anything or any person. So, when we get used to seeing objects, we recognize them, and when we look at them again, they are familiar; but, what about the objects that we have never seen and don't recognize? They could be standing directly in front of us, dead or alive, and we just don't see or hear them.

When we don't see, or hear objects that are directly in front of us, it makes them different and foreign. Therefore, if there are planets in our galaxy or not that have life on them, and that life somehow made it to Earth, we may not recognize it as something familiar. Even if we did, our governments will have more access to it or them, and based on national security concerns, or some other reason, will not volunteer any information.

We have to understand that we don't know everything about our world, and if you think you do, or you follow the directions of people who say they do, then you are mistaken. So, to answer the question of whether there is life outside of this world, we must refer to history.

Some of our greatest leaders indicated that we must prepare ourselves for battle with adversaries from outside of this world. What do they mean? Come on! To avoid the term naïve, governments have information about the things to which you and I are not accustomed. So, why did these leaders mention the term "outside of this world?"

www.ingramcontent.com/pod-product-compliance
Lightning Source LLC
Chambersburg PA
CBHW020348290526
45785CB00005B/2186